IMAGES
of England

WEST DRAYTON
AND YIEWSLEY

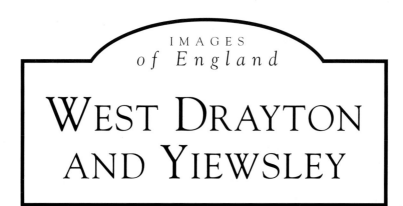

IMAGES
of England

WEST DRAYTON
AND YIEWSLEY

James Skinner

To Beverley,
Best wishes, James Skinner

TEMPUS

You "Auto" come to   YIEWSLEY

In spite of the obvious pun, if this early 1900s postcard, originally printed in colour, didn't attract visitors to Yiewsley, what else would?

Frontispiece: What the well-dressed Yiewsley family was wearing in the early 1920s: Eliza Hart with two of her children pose in their Sunday best.

This book is dedicated to my daughters, Susan and Lisa

First published 2003

Tempus Publishing Limited
The Mill, Brimscombe Port,
Stroud, Gloucestershire, GL5 2QG

British Library Cataloguing in Publication Data.
A catalogue record for this book is available from the British Library.

ISBN 0 7524 2841 1

Typesetting and origination by Tempus Publishing Limited.
Printed in Great Britain by Midway Colour Print, Wiltshire.

Contents

This could easily be a scene from the Will Hay comedy *Where's That Fire?* In fact it is the old Harmondsworth fire engine brought out of retirement for the West Drayton Coronation Procession in 1937. Manning it are, left to right, G. Hockley, A. Tasker, W. Devonshire, D. Grey and H. Bateman.

Acknowledgements

My sincere thanks are due to the following for their help in the researching of this book, and also for the loan of their photographs and other material:

Carolynne Cotton and Gwyn Jones – Heritage Department, Uxbridge Central Library, Audrey Beasley, Jack Stevenson, Vera Caiger, Pauline Burton, Max Gittins, Peter Bayley, Vic Brown, Ted Eggleston, Brian Moores, Terry Cluny, John Byrne, Marcy Marshall, Jack Dubrey, Jim Langley, David Shute, Don Mead, Don Taylor, Rose Emerton, Eileen and Douglas Rust, Elaine Bodenham, Peter Prunty, Denis Josey, Kay Hunt, Ken Pearce, Michael Craxton, Audrey Skinner, Julian Rhind-Tutt, Carla Mendonca, Ron Southby, Sharon Clayton and Tony Thrasher.

Thanks also to Yogie James Trivedy for his assistance in processing the manuscript, and a special thank you to Dr R.T. Smith for allowing me access to the archives of Yiewsley and West Drayton History Society.

Finally, I am indebted to the *Uxbridge Gazette* for granting permission to reproduce their photographs throughout this book, and to Mark Sherman Athletics Images for permission to use the pictures on page 60.

Introduction

The history of West Drayton and Yiewsley, from the tenth century through to the era of the Lords of the Manor, the Pagets and De Burghs, has already been admirably documented in the works of local historians A.H. Cox and S.A.J. McVeigh. This book, therefore, is not intended to be a history, but rather a retrospective look into the more recent past, that is the last 150 years or so, and to concern itself more with the social and community life of the two towns.

In his book *Greater London – a Narrative of its History, its People and its Places*, published around 1880, Edward Walford described West Drayton thus:

> Drayton, written 'Draitone' in the Domesday Book, is a large, irregular village on the western border of Middlesex. The parish is separated on its western side from Buckinghamshire by the River Colne, which meanders peacefully along through meadows and cornfields, and having here and there upon its banks a mill or a farmyard. Out of the way of turmoil and strife, the place has apparently enjoyed from its earliest period, an existence of peaceful retirement and seclusion.

Well, that was one man's opinion! Some years earlier, in 1838, *The Mirror* magazine published a letter from a visitor to West Drayton in which he wrote:

> Wending our way beneath the elms which shaded the road, we arrived at the village green, upon which geese, pigs and donkeys were grazing with all the felicity of rural security.

Pastoral scenes of a similar nature were also a feature of Yiewsley (known originally as 'Wiuesleg'). The village was virtually a continuation of West Drayton – that is until it was separated from its neighbour by the cutting of the canal in 1771, and the construction of the railway in 1837. The Yiewsley landscape was composed of farms, golden cornfields flecked with red poppies, and meadows decked with buttercups and bluebells. A shallow stream (the River Pinn) lazily wound its way through this rural setting, completing the picture. Both villages presented idyllic images of a much gentler, bygone age when life was lived at a more leisurely pace, but not everything in this garden was lovely. Poverty abounded throughout the area; paupers were much in evidence and a workhouse was built near The Green in 1807, followed by the advent of soup kitchens.

Later there were changes in the landscape. Yiewsley was found to be rich in brick earth, and three brickfields were opened in the areas around Trout Road, Falling Lane and adjacent Starveall. It has been recorded that much of nineteenth-century London was built of bricks from this district. Eventually, agriculture gave way to brick making, and when the fields were finally worked out in the mid-1930s, the gravel and ballast companies moved in and a new industry began. Today, the whole of the former Starveall area is occupied by Stockley Business Park.

In West Drayton, industry had been confined mainly to milling and brewing. The mill dated from the eleventh century, and produced corn, barley, malt and then paper and millboard, until being gutted by fire in 1913. The brewery had closed in 1911. Then, after the First World War ended in 1918, a range of factories sprang up throughout the area, most of them sited in Yiewsley.

When they weren't working, local people appear to have made the most of their free time, and during the last century engaged in a number of leisure activities. In addition to the clubs and societies described within these pages, there were many others that played a prominent part in social life – notably Yiewsley Bowling Club, some of whose members represented the county. The club enjoyed the facilities of two fine Cumberland turf greens, the first being laid in 1929. While back in the 1860s, there was a string band, a drum and fife band, a minstrel troupe, and, by 1923, a radio society, a canine society and a glee club. Add to these the working mens' club, British Legion, Rotary Club, Community Association and a new cinema, and some might think it was all play and no work!

Today, newcomers to the area would need vivid imaginations to envisage the rural landscapes described earlier and they would be hard pressed to picture West Drayton as a centre of culture, but surely during the latter part of the nineteenth and early part of the twentieth centuries, it was just that. The Green in particular, with so many elegant period houses around its borders, appears to have been a favourite haven for actors, authors and artists. The fact that there were also five public houses in close proximity was, probably, quite coincidental! But no doubt the new residents appreciated that there was another advantage to living in West Drayton – they could commute from London by train in eighteen minutes – a feat which in no way could be accomplished today!

By way of a postscript, there are a few items that could not be included in the book, but are certainly worthy of mention. The first concerns West Drayton's most famous visitor – Good Queen Bess, the Virgin Queen. Elizabeth I was entertained for some days at the Manor House in October 1602 by her cousin, Lord Hunsdon. While the most infamous was surely William Joyce (dubbed 'Lord Haw Haw' during the Second World War) who, in his capacity as Director of Propaganda for Sir Oswald Mosley's British Union of Fascists, addressed a meeting at St Martin's Hall in June 1936. Subsequently, he was challenged to a debate by local schoolmaster Tom Gittins, but sent a deputy in his stead. However, there were more welcome visitors, among them Karl Marx's daughter Eleanor, who, in September 1890, was the first woman to make a speech on The Green when she spoke in support of strikes by the Brickmakers' Union.

Finally, on a lighter note, mention must be made of two of the town's brightest stars – current personalities, both of whom were born and bred in Yiewsley. The first needs no introduction – he is Ronnie Wood of the Rolling Stones and is one of three brothers who are all musicians and artists. The second is Paula Wood (no relation), a champion swimmer who has won the National Open Water Championships for six consecutive years from 1997 to 2002.

One
Town and Country

A corner of West Drayton Green that has hardly changed during several centuries. Originally a swamp that was drained at the end of the sixteenth century, The Green is one of the largest in Middlesex. It was the centre of village life and the venue for countless celebrations including Coronations and Royal Jubilees, annual May Day and Empire Day festivities and Guy Fawkes night processions and bonfires. The building on the left is Avenue House.

Farms and smallholdings remained a major part of the Yiewsley landscape long after the opening of the brickfields. Agriculture was still an important industry in 1930, when this picture was taken of sea-kale being planted on Philpott's farm.

Another rural scene off Money Lane, West Drayton, featuring female pickers at Reamsbottom & Company's seed factory in 1935. The ladies include Nell Phillips, Lilian Aubrey, Edith Josey, Hilda Manley and Kit Bristow.

This early eighteenth-century inn in Trout Road, Yiewsley, was still a scene of tranquillity in the 1930s. Originally known as The Chequers, then The Trout and finally The Trout and Chequers, it closed in 1950 and was subsequently demolished.

Fortunately, some serenity still prevails in the area, as depicted in this view of the River Frays in a quiet backwater behind Money Lane, West Drayton.

Swan Road, West Drayton, *c.* 1900. The mansion on the left was Drayton House (formerly The Burroughs), part of an estate dating from the fifteenth century. It became known as Stacy's Park when purchased by W.S. Stacy in the late nineteenth century, and was sold in 1923 when the mansion was demolished. On the extreme right is the eighteenth-century house, Swains, most of which has survived.

Swan Road in 1931, photographed from almost the same spot as the picture above. The houses are the result of Drayton House estate development. Local baker M.E. Rumble's horse-drawn van is on the right. He traded from a shop further down the road throughout most of the twentieth century.

Colham Avenue, Yiewsley. Originally a branch of the canal known as Otter Dock, used for transporting bricks from the nearby brickfields, it was filled in and an avenue of trees planted in 1910. The roads on either side – Ernest Road and Dock Road – were renamed Colham Avenue in 1938.

Ferrers Avenue, West Drayton on a bleak, wintry day in the 1950s. The road was constructed through the centre of the former Drayton House estate in the mid-twenties, and named after a previous owner, Robert – the sixth Earl Ferrers.

Yiewsley High Street in the 1920s. The former Wesleyan chapel can be seen on the left.

Yiewsley High Street in the mid-1930s, pictured from the old Colham Bridge. Harris's Drapery and the adjoining shops were sited where the Medical Centre now stands. A billboard for the Regal Cinema, Uxbridge, can be seen further along the street.

Colham Bridge in 1933, photographed from the West Drayton side. When the bridge and road were widened in 1939, the Anchor public house was set further back.

The same location viewed from the Yiewsley side.

Station Road, West Drayton, at the junction of Swan Road in 1935. The large building on the left – the then new post office, had opened two years earlier.

Almost a country scene in the middle of town where the new Colham Bridge spans the Grand Union Canal (formerly the Grand Junction). Although not the official boundary, the waterway separates Yiewsley from West Drayton.

Two
Bricks and Mortar

Wooden Row – a group of cottages at Stockley (known as Starveall until 1912). Nicknamed 'Rabbit Hutch Row' by the locals, they were situated between the canal and the railway tracks and built for families working in the brickfields. Starveall had its own schoolhouse and mission hall, and local nonagenarian Fred 'Banjo' Wheeler, whose mother was one of the 'brickies', remembers attending both. Wooden Row was demolished during the 1930s as part of the slum clearance scheme.

Built during the reign of Henry VIII, St George's Meadows, Mill Road, West Drayton underwent several structural changes during the past four centuries. Originally called Palmers, then Woodpecker Farm when owned by writer Henry Havelock Ellis, it was renamed Old Meadows by wealthy American socialite Emilie Grigsby, who purchased the property in 1913. She entertained many famous figures including Yeats, Rodin and Rupert Brooke, while Lord Kitchener and Sir John French held a secret conference there during the First World War. When she died in 1964, Emilie, who was born on St George's Day, bequeathed the house to the National Trust, requesting that it be renamed St George's Meadows. Previously, in 1926, she donated a statue of her patron saint to St Catherine's church on The Green.

Opposite above: Staff and patrons line up in front of The Royal Oak at the northern end of Yiewsley High Street, *c*. 1900. The building was demolished during the 1960s to make way for road widening.

Opposite below: Bordered by the narrow River Pinn, and known originally as Brookside, the Grange is a seventeenth-century building situated just beyond the site of the former Royal Oak. The house was extensively altered during the eighteenth century, and its original timber framing is now encased in brick. Purchased by George Wynn in the 1890s, it was inherited by his granddaughter, Sylva Kingham, who lived there throughout her married life. A grade-II listed building, it has now been converted into offices. In 1937, the GWR named one of its engines (No.6859) after the house, calling it *Yiewsley Grange*.

The official opening of the Church Army Houses in Horton Road, Yiewsley in October, 1933.

Council Chairman F.E. Dominey presenting Mrs Catlin with the keys to her new house – No. 32 Providence Road – at the opening of Yiewsley Homes for the Aged in March 1934.

The De Burgh Arms, High Street, Yiewsley, in the 1950s. A listed building dating from the seventeenth century, it underwent many alterations over the years, but has remained unchanged since 1920. In 1953, it featured prominently in the film Genevieve in scenes where Kenneth More, Dinah Sheridan, John Gregson and Kay Kendall sat on the front steps eating ice creams.

The Swan, Swan Road in 1950. Built in the sixteenth century, it was demolished in 1965, and eventually replaced with the present building.

Drayton Hall dates from the early nineteenth century, although a seventeenth-century mansion occupied the site previously. From 1786, it was the home of the De Burgh family, and Hubert De Burgh entertained Napoleon III there in 1872. The Hall housed a variety of tenants throughout the years, including a girls' school evacuated from Paris in the First World War. In 1925 it became a private hotel, and in 1952 the council's new headquarters. It is now used as commercial offices.

Built in 1881, these houses in De Burgh Crescent, Station Road, West Drayton appear much the same today.

Avenue House, situated in the south-eastern corner of The Green, dates from the eighteenth century. It was occupied by actor/cricketer C. Aubrey Smith from 1903 to 1908.

Old Orchard in Mill Road was built for C. Aubrey Smith when he vacated Avenue House. He maintained the property for many years even after moving to Hollywood in 1930. When it was eventually demolished, The Burroughs old peoples' home was erected on the site.

Various seventeenth-century buildings facing The Green as they are today. They include parts of the Britannia Brewery owned by the Thatcher family from 1805 to 1910; the King's Head and Britannia Tap public houses. Now converted into flats and offices, the complex preserves the name 'Britannia' in the form of an old inn sign (in the foreground).

Hope Cottage (left) facing The Green. Dating from the eighteenth century, it was owned originally by the Swift family. From the 1930s it was home to actor/author Reyner Barton and his wife Margaret. Both belonged to the Old Vic Company, and her brother was local artist Dudley Haynes. Rose Cottage (right) was occupied for a time in the 1890s by Father M. Wren, founder of St Catherine's church, and from 1930 by historian Maurice Bawtree and his wife Catherine (née Swift).

Southlands, a grade-II listed building next to Avenue House, began life as a Tudor farmhouse in the 1500s. An elegant Queen Anne frontage was added during the seventeenth century. From 1902 to 1911, it was occupied by Cosmo Hamilton, author of over forty plays and thirty novels, including *The Blindness of Virtue* – based on West Drayton and its characters. His wife, actress Beryl Faber, sister of C. Aubrey Smith, made her final West End appearance in a dramatised version of the book in 1912. Southlands was then home to the Davey family up until 1963, when it was acquired by the council for eventual use as an arts centre.

The Old House (extreme right) is a listed building facing The Green, and dates from the eighteenth century. It was known originally as Ivy Cottage. In the 1930s it was occupied by actor Henry Mollison, whose father William and brothers Clifford and William were all well known on the London stage. Henry, a POW for five years in the Second World War, returned to the theatre and also appeared in Ealing films *Whisky Galore* and *The Man in the White Suit*. Amy Johnson, world famous flier, was married to Jim Mollison, a relative of Henry's, and often stayed at the house during the 1930s. On the left of the picture can be seen the New House and the start of the Victorian terrace Daisy Villas, built in 1896.

West Drayton's former post office in Station Road, prior to its opening in June, 1933. A new automatic telephone exchange was incorporated in 1937/38, and extensions were added in 1962. It ceased to operate as a post office in 1997, and is now used for commercial purposes.

West Drayton Women's Institute Hall, The Green. Built in 1951 on the site of the former Vine House, a private boys' school, it was a gift from the Davey family to commemorate Hilda Davey's twenty-five years as president. The local branch was formed in 1919 and met at various venues until acquiring its own premises. A second building (right of picture) was erected in 1975 for use by the Middlesex Federation of WIs, but during the 1980s, the Institute was obliged to dispose of most of the main hall , which is now a medical centre.

Three
Local Government

Yiewsley and District Council Offices on the corner of High Street and Fairfield Road in 1928. The building was demolished in 1930, and replaced with a new Town Hall. The solitary policeman is one of two who served all of Yiewsley, although based in Uxbridge. The area had no police station of its own until 1964.

Councillors and staff of Yiewsley and West Drayton Urban District Council at the opening of the new Town Hall in May, 1930. F.E. Dominey (chairman) is sixth from the left in the front row, and other prominent members were W. Roberts (on his left) and Revd L.E. Prout, vicar of St Martin's, in the centre of the back row.

Yiewsley branch of the National Association of Local Government Officers (NALGO) and guests at their first annual dinner held at the Anglo Swiss Screw Company, Trout Road, on 13 March 1948.

Yiewsley and West Drayton councillors and Town Hall staff at their annual bowls match on the new green in Yiewsley Recreation Ground in the early 1950s. Evidently the council believed in the 'all work and no play' theory, and staged regular bowls and cricket matches in addition to indoor bowling tournaments.

Town Crier Charles Tamplin on the balcony of Yiewsley UDC offices, proclaiming the founding of the London Borough of Hillingdon on 1 April 1965. The new borough comprised the borough of Uxbridge and the councils of Hayes and Harlington, Ruislip-Northwood, as well as Yiewsley and West Drayton.

The last council meeting of the former Yiewsley and West Drayton UDC at Drayton Hall in 1965. When the old Town Hall offices proved inadequate, the local authority moved into this building in 1952. Dora Eggleton is in the chair, and mayor elect Terry Cluny is seated third from the left.

Terry Cluny, the second Mayor of Hillingdon Borough, accompanied by Clerk to the council George Hooper in wig and gown, is escorted by an RAF Regiment guard of honour. Long-time Yiewsley resident Mr Cluny is about to enter St Catherine's Roman Catholic church to attend a Civic Service known as 'Mayor's Sunday' on 19 June 1966. This was the second such service to be held in the church, the first being in 1958 for John Croly, the then chairman of the former UDC.

Four

Leisure
and Recreation

Outings organized by public houses for their regulars have always been a popular pastime. These are patrons of the George and Dragon in Yiewsley High Street, about to depart on a charabanc trip to Ascot races in 1927. The landlord Mr Rushbrook is the gentleman at the top of the picture.

Another 'pub' outing, *c.* 1930. This one from The Engine, Station Road, West Drayton relied on 'horse power' rather than mechanisation. Among the smartly-dressed gents were Messrs Sinfield, Pope, Brown, Bunn, Sirey, Barnes, Curling and Rolfe.

Still trusting in horses and brakes is this party from The King's Head, The Green, setting out for Ascot in 1935. The landlady, Mrs Caterer, is next to Fred Atkins (holding the name board), and others include Messrs Simpson, Gould, Brown and Merritt.

This West Drayton Girl Guides and Brownies group includes two Yiewsley sisters, Ruby and Alice Crockett. The company was formed on 12 June 1916, and by 1920 was captained by Dorothy Dymes who resigned in 1921.

The Guides in 1922, now captained by Constance Swift, former lieutenant to Miss Dymes.

West Drayton Boy Scouts in the early 1920s with their Scoutmaster and Revd A.W.S.A. Row, vicar of St Martin's.

The Guides netball team, c. 1921. Left to right, back row: Alice Daniels, Lizzie Simpson. Middle row: Agnes Mackenzie, Alice Crockett (captain), Rose Dyer. Front row: Winnie Watts, Phyllis Hempstead.

Times were hard during the Depression years of the 1930s, but there were occasional compensations in the way of 'treats' for the youngsters. Two examples were the 1933 Christmas Pantomime advertised above, at which all the children received a present, and (*below*) an 'Open-Air Treat' for 2,500 children at The Closes to celebrate the Silver Jubilee of King George V and Queen Mary in 1935, where every child was given a medal presented by the Middlesex County Council.

MARLBORO' CINEMA
YIEWSLEY
SPECIAL CHILDREN'S MATINEE

WEDNESDAY, DECEMBER 27th

DOORS OPEN 2 p.m.   Commencing 2.30 to 5 p.m.   MATINEE PRICES.
BALCONY SEATS BOOKABLE.

GRAND PANTOMIME
"PUSS IN BOOTS"

Mr. JACK ALLEN The Popular Children's Entertainer
OLIVER PAYNE & THEYER, Piano Accordionists, In Selections from their Repertoire
SNOOKUM'S CHRISTMAS PARTY
FREE GIFT TO EVERY CHILD

DON'T LET YOUR CHILDREN MISS THIS GREAT CHRISTMAS TREAT
PLENTY OF SEATS AT 6d. FOR THE CHILDREN.   STALLS 9d.   BALCONY 1/3
USUAL PROGRAMME AT 5.30 P.M.

Another treat for local children was this Christmas party at the Co-op Hall, Yiewsley, in 1936, generously provided by the Oddfellows Friendly Society. Among the guests were Audrey Bateman and her brother Joe.

Mrs Kathleen Lovibond, CBE, opening Yiewsley Conservative Association fête at the Recreation Ground in 1935. Mrs Lovibond became Mayor of Uxbridge in 1956/57.

Even firemen need to take time off occasionally, especially if the occasion is a colleague's wedding. This 1930s group features some of the Yiewsley Brigade outside their fire station in Yew Avenue. The happy couple are Mr and Mrs Ted Asby, and firemen W. Devonshire, G. Hockley, A. Tasker and H. Batemen are among those in attendance.

Councillor J.O. Fieldgate (third from right) with colleagues at the opening of West Drayton tennis courts at The Closes, Church Road in June 1934.

Children had to provide their own amusement in the 1920s and 1930s. These happy Yiewsley youngsters are enjoying themselves during the summer of 1932, in an improvised pool consisting of two tin baths.

Two years later, Yiewsley council provided them with the real thing – an open-air swimming pool off Otterfield Road, adjacent to the recreation ground. The pool was covered in 1976, and today boasts a complete leisure complex, incorporating a gym, steam room, sauna and solarium. A far cry from the days of the tin bath!

Yiewsley & West Drayton Boys' Club FC at Evelyn's Stadium in May 1944, after beating 'The Rest' (of the Minor League). Left to right, back row: R. Painter, R. Johnson, J. Fuller, W. Barnett, R. Beale (captain) J. Crockett, C. Jones. Front row: J. Stevenson (club leader), V. Brown, S. Grant, K. Painter, A. Dungate, S. Bennett, Mr Bennett (trainer). The club originated in 1938, under the auspices of the Toc H movement. Its first leader, Philip Penfold, was succeeded by his brother-in-law Jack Stevenson in 1940. Leading a nomadic existence, the club moved headquarters several times in its early years. A youth club with a difference, it not only provided facilities for every type of sport, but encouraged activities such as debating, drama, music, photography, gardening, chess and first aid. The boys had their own parliament and ran the club themselves under the leader's guidance, and his main aim always was to teach them good citizenship. He resigned in 1948 due to business commitments, and Mr R.W. Gardner took over in 1950, being succeeded by A. Marks in 1956. From 1953, the club has occupied a converted bungalow in Cherry Lane as its permanent home.

Boys' Club bicycle-polo team after a league match at Cowley in the early 1940s. Left to right: J. Stevenson, D. Hammond, W. Barnett, R. Eggleston, J. Watts, D. Horwood, J. Knowles.

Boys' Club members and their girl friends setting out from Money Lane on a cycling trip at Easter, 1946.

Boys' Club physical training team, with their instructor ex-RAF Flight Sergeant Bunker, *c.* 1946.

Staff from the Drayton Regulator & Instrument Company before setting out from Horton Road on the firm's annual outing in the summer of 1948. They were part of a large contingent conveyed by a fleet of coaches on a day trip to Southsea.

Another day trip – on this occasion organized by Yiewsley FC Supporters' Club, *c.* 1952. They appear to be in good spirits as they have lunch in the coach park of 'Glorious Goodwood' racecourse in Sussex.

Garden fêtes were still popular in the 1950s, and this one organized by Yiewsley and West Drayton Community Association was no exception. Television personality Jeanne Heal, who opened the fête, is pictured with council chairman George Gittins and Oscar Frey, founder of Anglo Swiss Screw Company. Local MP Frank Beswick was also present, as were over 2,000 members of the public. Other celebrities who opened fêtes in the area were Hollywood actress Binnie Barnes, television comedian Dickie Henderson and Irish boxer Jack Doyle.

The Teddy Bears Picnic, 1950s style. Evidently children were still happy making their own amusement, as shown by this little girl hosting a tea party in her garden at Otterfield Road, Yiewsley.

Yiewsley Old Peoples' Welfare Committee celebrating the 1953 Coronation at the Baptist schoolrooms. Mrs Lucy Cossum, who was ninety-nine years old, is sitting in front of George Gittins. Next to him are Arthur Boote, clerk to the council, and Mrs Gittins.

Lord Ted Willis (playwright and scriptwriter) opening Southlands Arts Centre on 3 June 1967. With Leslie and Joan Nind at the helm, the centre provided facilities for painting, pottery, lace making, tapestry, wood carving, music and drama. Music recitals featuring top artistes Iris Loveridge, Juan Martin and others were staged under the auspices of Drayton Recorded Music Circle, formed by Anthony Andrews. Local singer Phyllis Wood, chairman of the Circle for fifteen years, was responsible for bringing these leading musicians to Southlands and other venues in the town, and was honoured for her work by Hillingdon Arts Association in 1987. Sylva Kingham, a gifted sculptress and Arts Council founder member, is fifth from the right in the group addressed by Lord Willis.

Five

Sporting Life

TUESDAY, MAY 15. 1866.

WEST DRAYTON RACES
WHITSUNTIDE HOLIDAYS.

MONDAY &· TUESDAY, MAY 21st AND 22nd.

FIVE RACES EACH DAY, AND A MATCH FOR £200.

The Great Western Railway run 10 Special Trains each day from London.

West Drayton is Two Miles from Uxbridge.

The Race Course is about 100 yards from Drayton Station.

Front page announcement in the *Buckinghamshire Advertiser* of the Whitsun Race Meeting at West Drayton in 1866. The course was situated on what is now the Garden City, and occupied forty-two acres. 157 horses were entered for the advertised two-day meeting, most being offloaded at the station in Tavistock Road, led down a ramp (that still exists), under the bridge and along Colham Mill Road to the entrance. Bank holiday meetings attracted crowds of 10,000 each day, including many undesirables, and the course gained a reputation as one of the most notorious in the London area. Eventually condemned by the Jockey Club, it was closed down in 1879.

West Drayton Golf Course in 1915. The club opened in 1895, its eighty-acre site embracing part of the old racecourse and extending to West Drayton mill. Membership consisted mainly of London businessmen whose annual subscription was three guineas. The Garden City residential estate now occupies the site, one of its roads being named Fairway Avenue. The club closed during the First World War due to falling membership.

The former Colham Mill House as it is today, converted into apartments. Standing at the entrance to the golf course, it served as the clubhouse and also provided accommodation for the caddies. During the past fifty years it was used by Valentine Paint and Varnish Company and BASF Paints and Inks Ltd.

West Drayton Cricket Club at its Mill Road ground in 1902. Left to right, back row: E. Humbert (president), G. Mercer, G. Berry, R. Latham, F. Potter, ? Bentall. Middle row: G. Thornhill, W. Ratcliff, B. Reed, A.O. Williams (captain), H.S.O. Williams, T. Sirey, ? Curtiss. Front row: P. Taylor (scorer), J. Thornhill (umpire). The club originated in 1868 under the name West Drayton Britannia, and after playing at Stacy's Park and Dog Kennel Meadow, moved to Mill Road in the 1880s.

The club in 1905. Left to right, back row: G. Taylor, W. Williams, F. Potter, ? Leslie, G. Mercer, R. Latham. Middle row: B. Reed, C. Aubrey Smith, G. Berry, HSO Williams. Front row: Johnny Maskell, H. Turner, J. Bentall.

West Drayton Cricket Club in 1912. On the extreme right of the second row is C. Aubrey Smith and next to him Willie (Nigel) Bruce, both future Hollywood actors. Nigel's brother, Sir Michael Bruce, is on the right of the front row.

Colham Green Cricket Club, *c.* 1914. On the extreme right of the back row was Yiewsley resident Ernest Ogan, sports journalist and editor at Odhams Press. He was also a British draughts champion. The team played on the sports ground of the old Evelyn's private school, and another ground nearby was used by Stockley Cricket Club, formed in 1929.

West Drayton Cricket Club in 1926. Left to right, standing: T. Watson, C. Fletcher, E. Ashby, T. Ryan, A.O. Williams, H. Holland, F. Fuller, ? Heathcote, G. Thornhill (umpire). Seated: J. Goodman, G. Davey (captain), G. Belsey and Johnny Maskell, who became the best all-rounder in the club's history, scoring over 9,000 runs and taking over 1,000 wickets.

The club in 1934. The players include A. Stevens, E. Ashby, T. Ryan, A.O. Williams, L. Bateman, C. Fletcher, E. Hopkins (captain), R. Stone, J. Maskell, G. Platford, B. Moranne, E. Turnbull, N. Reed.

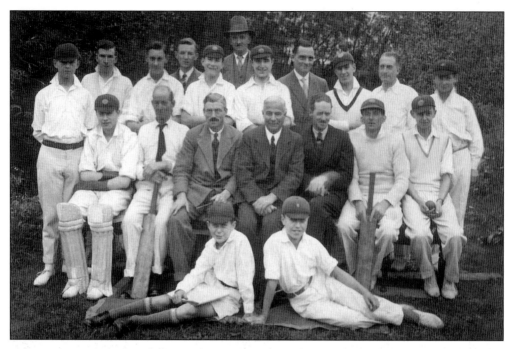

Garden City Cricket Club, seen here around 1930, was formed by residents of the new estate in 1924, and captained by A.E. Stevenson (seated second from the right). His son Jack is next to him and council chairman F.E. Dominey is in the centre. The members prepared the ground themselves on part of the old golf course, but moved to a new venue in Thorney Mill Road in the mid-thirties, eventually changing their name to Yiewsley-Drayton.

The Garden City Cricket Club annual dinner in March 1935, held at the Regal cinema, Uxbridge. Jack and Dorothy Stevenson are on the extreme left.

C. Aubrey Smith at West Drayton Cricket Club on Sunday 4 August, 1935. He had brought a team called the 'Thespids' to play his old club, and is seen here autographing a miniature bat for a young admirer. Although C. Aubrey did not play, the 'Thespids' won comfortably.

West Drayton Cricket Club, c. 1935. Over the years many local families contributed greatly to the club's success, among them the Williams', Daveys, Berrys and Fullers.

C. Aubrey Smith paid a return visit to the club in August 1938, and is seen here with two of the team's stalwarts A.O. Williams and Johnny Maskell. This was one of C. Aubrey's days off between filming *Sixty Glorious Years* and *The Four Feathers* at nearby Denham Studios.

AEL (Admiralty Engineering Laboratory) Cricket Club, c. 1939. Captain Jack Gardner is third from the left in the middle row, and former Garden City skipper A.E. Stevenson is on the extreme left of the same row. The club's private ground, opened in 1936, was part of the Admiralty premises in Warwick Road, West Drayton.

West Drayton Cricket Club, c. 1951/52. Peter Fuller (second from right) became the club's most prolific scorer, hitting in excess of 12,000 runs. His brother John exceeded 10,000, and their father Jack was a fine all-rounder. Jack Maskell (sitting second from right) played from 1937 to 1967, and in 1931 had captained Hayes FC in the Amateur Cup Final at Wembley. His brother was Dan Maskell, the international tennis player and commentator.

A happy occasion at the club in the early 1950s dubbed 'Past v. Present', when a team of 'old stagers' played the current eleven. Among the veterans were 'Pop' Ash, Jack Maskell, Jack Stevenson and 'Bunny' Moranne (who joined in 1928). Missing from the picture was long serving Alan Fincham, a member from 1949 to 1995.

The cricket club's presentation dinner in honour of Alan O. Williams at the Anglo Swiss Screw Company in the late 1940s. Long-term president Stuart Davey made the presentation in recognition of Alan's services to the club as captain and administrator since 1902. Donations to the testimonial fund were received from C. Aubrey Smith and Nigel Bruce. Nigel wrote 'Alan, his brothers and the West Drayton Cricket Club are all connected with some of the happiest days of my life.'

Yiewsley Football Club displaying junior league cups and medals won in 1913. Founded in 1872, the club entered senior football in 1919. After winning the Spartan League in 1949/50 and 1950/51, they progressed to the Delphian and Corinthian Leagues, before turning professional in 1958, when joining the Southern League. Managed originally by Jim Taylor and Bill Dodgin, the club signed Newcastle and England star Jackie Milburn as player/manager in 1961, and later a new road 'Milburn Drive' was named after him. The team's name was changed to Hillingdon Borough in 1965.

Yiewsley Football Club in their Spartan League days at Evelyn's Stadium, Falling Lane in 1949. Left to right, standing: Jim Taylor (coach), D. Brown, S. Lyddon, R. Cagney, E. Close, A. Cook, H. Marshall. Seated: E. Phillips, C. Harmes, R. Mathieson, G. Harvey, J. Burch.

'The Rest' (of the Yiewsley and West Drayton Minor League) after their defeat by the Boys' Club at Evelyn's Stadium in May 1944. The smiling youngster on the left of the front row is future England international Jim Langley.

Jim Langley in the Queens Park Rangers strip at Loftus Road during the mid-sixties, prior to returning to his home club as player/manager in 1967.

Yiewsley Athletic Football Club, winners of the Brentford & District League (Premier Division) in 1949/50. Captain Sid Palmer is holding the trophy.

Local hero Langley making one of his last appearances at Leas Stadium, Falling Lane, c. 1970. At the age of fourteen Jim was the youngest player to appear for Yiewsley. After army service, he signed for Guildford as a semi-pro, before moving to Leeds Utd, Brighton, Fulham (where he spent seven years and won three full England caps) and Queens Park Rangers. At forty-two, he was the oldest player to appear at Wembley when captaining his old team (now Hillingdon Borough) in the FA Trophy Final on 1 May 1971. Unfortunately, after leading 2-0 at half-time, Hillingdon lost 2-3.

YIEWSLEY FOOTBALL CLUB

Founded 1873

"Evelyns," Falling Lane, Yiewsley, Middx.   West Drayton 2948

SEASON - 1951-52

President - M. MULDER-CANTER, Esq.

Chairman:
G. BARKER, Esq., 5, Royal Lane, Yiewsley, Middx.

Vice-Chairman:
W. S. THORN, Esq., 70, Otterfield Road, Yiewsley, Middx.

General Secretary:
G. A. MOORE, Esq., 107, Staines Road, Feltham, Middx.

Treasurer and Press Secretary:
L. A. DOVE, Esq., 92, Otterfield Road, Yiewsley, Middx.

Match Secretary:
L. R. BOON, Esq., 53, Edgar Road, Yiewsley, Middx.

Assist. Match Secretary:
D. A. PORTER, Esq., 86 Hammond Road, Southall, Middx.

Team Manager
B. MIDDLETON, Esq., 41, North Road, Southall, Middx.

OFFICIAL PROGRAMME - THREEPENCE

AMATEUR CUP
1st Qualifying Round

Saturday, October 6th   Kick-off 3 p.m.

Yiewsley v. Carshalton Athletic

NEXT HOME GAME:

Saturday, October 13th   Kick-off 3.15 p.m.

To be announced

The holder of the Lucky Number Programme will receive Two Free Tickets for the Marlborough Cinema (available Monday to Friday next week), kindly presented by the Cinema Management.

GILLINGHAM FOOTBALL CLUB

OFFICIAL PROGRAMME
PRICE 3D

GILLINGHAM

Versus

YIEWSLEY

WED., 21st NOV. 1956 F.A. Cup Comp. 1st Round (Replay) K.O. 2 p.m.

TAXIS — 24-hour Service — TAXIS
J. BICKNELL MOTORS Ltd.
77a Gillingham Rd.,   58 Canterbury St.,
Gillingham : Kent
Ring 5431 Day Service   1169 Day & Night Service
LONG DISTANCE OUR SPECIALITY
Private Hire   Coach Automobile Engineers
WEDDINGS COASTAL TRIPS LONDON THEATRES
ANYWHERE   ANYTIME

J. W. LEECH & SONS LTD.
BUILDERS AND DECORATORS
47 KING STREET : ROCHESTER
Telephone : 2662

YOU MAY RELY UPON IT
IT'S PERFECT !

MULTI·BROADCAST
Interference Free Radio
Reception

Programme covers for some of Yiewsley FC's cup-ties from 1951 to their Wembley appearance twenty years later under the new name of Hillingdon Borough.

FOR GOOD READING
PENGUIN BOOKS
HARMONDSWORTH , MIDDLESEX

Self Drive and Chauffeur Driven Cars
AIR ENTERPRISES (London) LTD.
120 BATH ROAD HARLINGTON, Middx. 'Phone: HAYes 2433
NEW STANDARD CARS
Drive Yourself Hire from £2-10-0 per week   24 Hour Service

YIEWSLEY F.C.

LEAS STADIUM, FALLING LANE, YIEWSLEY, MIDDLESEX
Tel: West Drayton 2948

Official Programme
THREEPENCE

Chairman:
A. E. WHITTIT, Esq.

Hon. Gen. Secretary:
D. A. T. GRIMMETT, Esq.
Coneycote Lodge, Uxbridge Rd., Hillingdon, Middx.
Tel: Uxbridge 2817

CORINTHIAN   **LEAGUE**

Horton Road
West Drayton
Middlesex

MONO
CONCRETE CO. LTD.

Telephone :
West Drayton
2607

Telephone: West Drayton 3470
SHEATHER & CASE
Sheet Metal Workers, Tinsmiths, Welding and General Engineers
105 (REAR) STATION ROAD, WEST DRAYTON, MIDDX.

Try MILLERS FIRST
... most People do
MILLERS
THE POPULAR OUTFITTER
YIEWSLEY
OPPOSITE THE CO-OP

F.A. CHALLENGE TROPHY COMPETITION

FINAL

HILLINGDON BOROUGH
VERSUS
TELFORD UNITED

SATURDAY, 1st MAY, 1971   Kick-off 3 p.m.

WEMBLEY
EMPIRE   STADIUM

OFFICIAL PROGRAMME   10p

The 'Three R's' Football Club (First and Second Elevens) displaying trophies won in the 1965 season. The teams were comprised mainly of staff from the Road Machines Group of companies, although several ex-Yiewsley FC players were included in the squad.

Civic reception at Yiewsley council offices in 1948 for the Chefs de Mission and senior camp officials stationed at West Drayton Olympic Centre. The visitors and 700 athletes were housed at the RAF camp while preparing for the Olympics. Chairman of the council W. Roberts JP, seated third from the right, presided over the function.

West Drayton athlete Don Taylor setting the UK 10,000 metres record for Great Britain against West Germany at White City in 1963, in a time of twenty-eight minutes. 52.4 seconds. Don was ranked fourth in the world over this distance, and held the record until 1965. Also ranked fifth in the world over 3,000 metres, he represented Great Britain, England and London while competing in Belgium, Brazil, France, Hungary, Norway and Yugoslavia. At Sao Paulo, Brazil in 1963/64, he finished fifth in a field of 400, when running for Great Britain in the prestigious 'Round the Houses' race on New Years Eve.

Don Taylor winning the 1963 Southern Counties Three-Miles Championship at Harlow, Essex, beating European Champion Bruce Tulloch into second place.

Six
The Age of Steam

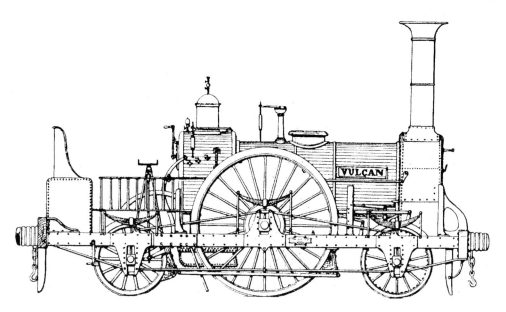

Line drawing of the *Vulcan* engine, designed to the specifications of Isambard Kingdom Brunel, the GWR's Chief Engineer. In November, 1837, the *Vulcan* and another engine, the *Premier*, were shipped from Liverpool via London Docks to the canal at West Drayton where they were hauled on to the railway tracks between Horton Bridge and the station. Then history was made when *Vulcan* became the first locomotive to use the GWR as it completed a successful mile and a half trial run down the line. Later, in June 1838, West Drayton was the first station to open on the line from Paddington.

West Drayton station in the early 1900s. Opened in 1879, it replaced the first one in Tavistock Road. In this rural setting horses and carriages await the arrival of passengers.

An express from Paddington passing through the station during the 1950s. The station name board reads 'West Drayton & Yiewsley – Junction for Uxbridge & Staines'. But in 1962 Dr Beeching's axe fell on the Uxbridge branch line, and the Staines line met the same fate in 1965.

Looking east towards Paddington from the 'up-relief' platform at West Drayton.

An Uxbridge branch line 'push and pull' train taking on water near the 'back-road platform' at West Drayton in August, 1951. The locomotive number is 0-4-2, tank no.1443.

In 1963, when this picture was taken, the figure of a ticket collector at the top of the stairs at West Drayton station was still a familiar sight, which has long since disappeared.

West Drayton railway bridge around 1959, before the road was lowered to enable double-decker buses to run underneath, and the bridge completely restructured.

Mr Frank Potter, who lived at the nineteenth-century house Elruge in Mill Road, was Station Master at West Drayton from 1885 to 1888. Mr Potter was promoted to the General Manager's Office at Paddington, where he eventually became General Manager of the GWR from 1912 until his death in 1919.

A carpet of snow on the tracks gives a wintry feel to this shot of a Paddington-bound express about to pass through the station, *c.* 1950. The building on the left is the listed Railway Arms public house.

Station master Conrad Salmon (left) with long-serving guard Walter Cooper, who was about to make his final journey from Uxbridge Vine Street station to West Drayton (before retiring from the GWR). Mr Salmon was appointed station master at Uxbridge in 1930, where he spent nine years before taking charge at West Drayton until his death in March 1948.

Seven

Two World Wars

Yiewsley brothers Bill and Arthur Crockett with a soldier friend (centre) before going off to war in 1915. Another brother also joined the army, and fortunately all three survived, although the two in the picture were wounded.

Programme cover of one of the regular Memorial Services held in Yiewsley after the end of the First World War. From a total of 530 men from Yiewsley and Stockley, 131 perished, while West Drayton's dead numbered forty-one.

RAF Reception Depot, Porters Way, West Drayton in 1936. It was one of several camps for the intake of new recruits, and during the First World War parts of the barracks were occupied by the RN Air Service. In the Second World War, it was overshadowed by neighbouring RAF Uxbridge, which as HQ No.11 Group, Fighter Command, played a vital role in the Battle of Britain. From 1952, the station accommodated many United States Army Air Force personnel, but they and most of the British airmen were posted during the 1960s. By 1971, the camp had been taken over by the then new Air Traffic Control Centre.

Only twenty-five years on from the 'war to end all wars', and another local family sees its three sons enlist in the forces. Mr and Mrs Eggleston of West Drayton, with sons Reg, Ted and Cyril in 1943. All three came through unscathed.

Yiewsley coal merchant J. Barber lends his lorry to aid a recruitment drive for the AFS (Auxiliary Fire Service) in 1939.

War Weapons Week, 1940. Home Guard 'D' Company, 1st Battalion 'X' zone turning into Church Road from The Green, forms part of a big parade through the town.

Yiewsley and West Drayton Silver Band heading the procession, followed by a detachment from the RAF.

The Home Guard reaches Station Road. Its commander was Guy Bolton, a schoolmaster in the area since 1910, and two of the younger marchers were Jack Dubrey and Ted Eggleston – both waiting to join the army.

West Drayton Home Guard displaying its trophies (presumably for marksmanship) in 1940. In the early days of the Second World War, 'Dad's Army' included quite a number of young men, awaiting call-up into HM Forces.

Another parade waiting to start from The Green. This time it's the turn of the ARP (Air Raid Precautions) First Aid Squad volunteers, in helmets and raincoats on a gloomy day in 1940.

On a brighter day, the ARP men are on the march again, with many of the volunteers at the rear of the column still awaiting uniforms.

Civil Defence ambulances lined up in Yiewsley Recreation Ground, *c.* 1940. The vehicles were presented to the council 'through the generosity of local factories and commercial undertakings'.

Now they have the staff to operate them. The man is outnumbered 10-1 by the female drivers and attendants employed on war work due to the manpower shortage.

Mrs Winifred Southby, her sons Ronald and John and their dog at the entrance to the Anderson air-raid shelter in their garden at Winnock Road, Yiewsley, *c.* 1940.

Pupils at Evelyn's school, Yiewsley, in 1940, being instructed how to use a stirrup pump to extinguish incendiary bombs.

Men preparing allotments at The Closes, as the 'Dig for Victory' campaign gets under way, c. 1940. In 1943, the local authority won the Viscount Bledisloe Cup for making the greatest contribution to the campaign during that year, and the Duke of Norfolk visited the town to present the trophy at a public meeting.

The lighter side of war. Girls love dressing up and this Yiewsley eleven-year-old was no exception as she posed in her father's ARP Warden's helmet and uniform, c. 1940.

Bomb damage at St Catherine's Rectory, Money Lane. On Saturday 16 November 1940, West Drayton was subjected to a concentrated incendiary bomb attack, and several buildings suffered damage. That same night, the RAF dropped 2,000 bombs on the city of Hamburg.

A week earlier on 10 November, the Black Bull Inn, Falling Lane, Yiewsley, received a direct hit and the rear of the building was demolished. Although many of the Sunday night customers were injured, fortunately there were no fatalities. Nearby cottages and houses opposite also suffered from the blast.

VE Day in May 1945 was the signal for nationwide celebrations, even though the war with Japan did not end until August. Street parties like this one outside The Cherry Tree public house, West Drayton, were the order of the day.

On a larger scale, this party took place in the playground of St Catherine's school, Money Lane, and children, parents, friends and neighbours were all invited.

This street party in Drayton Gardens was given by the residents for the youngsters living there.

The same party – later that evening. Some of the residents were musicians including young Brian Moores on the piano. The conductor (back to camera) was Councillor George Gittins.

Eight
Trade and Industry

Lunch break in the Starveall brickfields, *c.* 1897. James Crockett (second from right) with son Fred (sitting next to him), daughter Nancy (in the straw boater) and a fellow worker (centre). Nancy, a juvenile, was working illegally as many children did while playing truant from local schools. The two children sitting at the front are not known.

Knowle's boot and shoe shop, High Street, Yiewsley in the early 1900s.

The proprietor of the shop, W.H. Knowles, who traded there from 1906 until his death in 1950. A Middlesex County Councillor for three years, he was also a member of the Urban District Council. He and his wife were prominent Methodists, and he was mainly responsible for the formation of the Yiewsley & West Drayton Brotherhood in 1912.

William Sydney Belch's general shop, No.2 Bath Villas, High Street, Yiewsley in 1908. Described as 'Fancy Stores', the shop sold groceries, confectionery, toys, stationery and china and glassware that could also be hired. In addition, it advertised a picture-framing service and the serving of luncheons and teas.

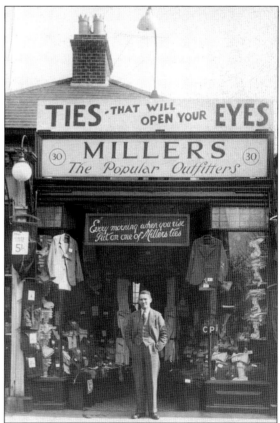

Rendle Dubrey in front of his outfitters shop in Yiewsley High Street in 1928. He purchased it for £550 in 1925 from Mr and Mrs Miller and retained the original name. His son Jack eventually took over the business, and when it closed in 1986, 'Millers' had greatly extended, owning three adjacent shops in addition to the original.

A 1953 advertisement for the Yiewsley & West Drayton Co-op which was taken over by the London CWS Ltd in the early 1930s. The Yiewsley society was formed in 1896; the building enlarged in 1913; and again in 1934. It incorporated a large hall on the first floor, used regularly for various functions and meetings.

The Co-operative complex, High Street, Yiewsley after its closing down sale in 1976. Subsequently it was demolished and a supermarket erected in its place. Initially trading under various names, it is now known simply as Yiewsley Co-op.

Johnson's Wax Company on the canal side at Colham Wharf, Yiewsley, in the early 1930s. The factory opened in 1919 and closed in 1960, when the company moved to Frimley. In 1982, the older buildings were demolished in favour of an office block that incorporates the original name plaque inscribed 'Colham Wharf 1796' in its front wall.

Workers from Johnson's Wax Company during a lunch break in 1941. They were photographed on the roof of an annexe (still standing) to the original building. Audrey Bateman is the girl standing on the extreme left.

THE POWER PLANT CO. LTD.
WEST DRAYTON · MIDDLESEX · ENGLAND

GOOD MIXING

essential in concrete !

THE MONO CONCRETE COMPANY
since its origin in a small shed in Yiewsley in 1925 has expanded until to-day it has one of the largest concrete works in Southern England, covering 16 acres of land, four of which are covered by factories and casting shops.

THIS DEVELOPMENT
has been due mainly to the introduction of special machinery for constructing concrete pipes—pipes for all types of drainage, sewerage, wells, manholes, etc.

IN THE PAST
concrete was treated as a substitute . . . .
. . . . to-day it is being used as the most suitable material for the job!

THE NAME
of the Company—MONO— was derived from the fact that this was one of the first firms to manufacture the socket and the barrel of a concrete pipe in one operation.

MONO CONCETE

COMPANY LTD.

WEST DRAYTON

Advertisements for four local industrial concerns. Others included Bux Corrugated Containers, Hardun's, C.V. Creffield, Valentine's Paints, Wilkins Campbell, Rotary Photographic Company which operated from 1900 to 1951, and Yiewsley Carpet Company (1932 to 1961).

Anglo-Swiss Screw Co. Ltd.

(Established in Yiewsley since 1919)

MAKERS OF

PRECISION SCREWS, NUTS
AND TURNED PARTS

offer

Loyal Greetings

to

Her Majesty

QUEEN
ELIZABETH II

on the occasion of

Her Coronation

June 2nd, 1953

From the West Drayton factory of Drayton Regulator & Instrument Co., Ltd., flows an unending stream of equipment to every corner of the world. Electric motors to the U.S.A. . . . steam traps to New Zealand . . . heating and ventilating equipment to Aden . . . dye vat controllers to the U.S.S.R. And, of course, throughout the British Isles, factories, nuclear and electrical power stations, hospitals, transport, collieries and large buildings depend on Drayton for steam traps and steam accessories, controllers and instruments for industrial and space heating applications, fractional h.p. geared motor units, and metal bellows and bellows assemblies.

THE DRAYTON REGULATOR & INSTRUMENT CO., LTD.
HORTON ROAD · YIEWSLEY · WEST DRAYTON · MIDDLESEX

Part of the electrical assembly bay.

A corner of the machine shop.

The workforce of Drayton Regulator & Instrument Company at the Horton Road factory in 1936. The company and its subsidiaries operated for some sixty years, and closed in 1980, by then known as Drayton Controls.

Mayor Terry Cluny visiting the Power Plant factory, Kingston Lane, West Drayton in 1965. The company's managing director is standing second from the left.

A 1953 advertisement for the Road Machines Company, Horton Road, Yiewsley.

W.M. (Bill) Robb, a Scotsman married to a local girl, founded Road Machines, Ltd in 1946. Starting with a staff of seven of his friends, Mr Robb built up a successful international company within a few years, securing government and local authority contracts followed by a vast export trade. He also established a building business with offices on the same site, at Horton Parade.

Nine
Schooldays

Pupils of West Drayton Primary school with headmistress Mrs M.M. Turner (on the extreme left). The school opened on 26 August 1905, next to the National school in Station Road, whose headmaster was Mrs Turner's husband. Mrs Turner retired in 1921 and in 1979 the school moved into part of the former St Martin's school in Kingston Lane.

Pupils of St Matthew's Church of England school, High Street, Yiewsley, *c.* 1911. The school opened in 1872, and is still thriving today.

Providence Road school, Yiewsley, as it is today. Opened in 1905, it closed in 1981 but has since re-opened as a Pupil Referral Unit known as Hillingdon Tuition Centre.

Side view of St Stephen's school, Yiewsley. Opened in 1906, it closed in 1979, and pupils were transferred to the adjacent St Matthew's.

Diamond Jubilee celebrations at St Stephen's school in 1966. Guest of honour was Mayor Terry Cluny, whose wife Betty is cutting the anniversary cake.

Boys working in the carpenter's shop of Padcroft Boys' Home, Yiewsley, in 1933. Padcroft was originally a private college, opened in 1875. It was purchased by the Church of England Temperance Society in 1900 as a boys' home and later transferred to the London Police Court Commission, who closed it in 1949. From the outset, Frank Green was its only manager. After closure, the buildings and playing fields were acquired by the Middlesex County Council for use as a community centre.

Physical training display at Evelyn's school, Yiewsley in 1937, also presented at the Ideal Home Exhibition at Olympia. Opened on 11 March 1936, Evelyn's was labelled 'a senior modern school for boys and girls' and described as 'an educational palace'. Although it already accommodated 900 pupils, it was enlarged in 1972.

Evelyn's school football team in 1938. Left to right, back row: G. Brawn, A. Nicholls, W. Tomlinson, W. Bull, R. Dymock, G. Puddle. Front row: R. Dickenson, D. Goodenough, P. Bayley, ? Cotton, R. Batley.

Senior prefects of Evelyn's in 1939. On the right end of the front row is Peter Bayley, future West Drayton cricketer and Uxbridge magistrate.

Pupils from St Catherine's Roman Catholic school, West Drayton, accompanied by parents processing to the church for the annual ceremony of crowning the lady statue , in May, 1933. At this time, the pupils were housed in an 1868 building in Money Lane, and it was not until 1939 that a new school was opened nearby.

St Catherine's school netball team at Uxbridge & District Primary schools rally in March, 1992. Left to right, back row: R. Dawson, C. Fitzgerald, C. Levell, N. Warren, L. Reed. Front row: E. Topping, L. Coughlin, S. Longman, L. Murphy. Beaten in the semi-final, the team had previously finished runners-up in the league. The school has a fine record in netball, and from 1968 to 1972, won the league championship four times in addition to the Borough rally.

Ten

Treading the Boards

Members of the Yiewsley Concert Party, *c.* 1914. Second from the left is Nancy Jackson; the others are unknown. Music and dramatic societies (including school and church groups) had been in existence locally since the late 1800s and, up to 1914, the West Drayton Mummers' play was performed annually.

West Drayton Players presenting *The Cup of Happiness* at the Church Room, Cowley in December 1933. Founded in 1929 by former professional actress Peggy Ross, the group gave many charity performances, this one being in aid of Cowley Nursing Fund.

The Players' production of *If Four Walls Told* again staged at Cowley in December 1937. This scene includes three sisters Pauline, Marie and Yvonne Moranne, and Charles Cox, E.W. Thorne, Nancy and Annie Bowyer, Joy Williams, A.E. Allson and F. Bignell.

The Return of the Prodigal performed by the Players at St Martin's Hall, West Drayton in 1930. Producer Peggy Ross is seated on the extreme left.

One of the Players' last productions – *This Blessed Plot* at St Catherine's school in December, 1949. Left to right: Marie Moranne, Simone Bush (sitting), Douglas Beale, Jack Davis, Peter Fuller.

Tir Nan Og (Land of Youth) Players, West Drayton performing *Murder Party* at St Catherine's school, *c.* 1949. They were a youth group, formed in around 1942 and comprised mainly of St Catherine's old scholars, their producer being the headmaster's wife, Gertrude McVeigh. Left to right: D. Fitzgibbon, A. Gordon, M. Twomey, J. Twomey, J. Hearst, W. Twomey, D. Gage, M. Sweeney, P. Hamey.

The Tir Nan Og group preparing to leave for Holbeach, Lincolnshire, where they participated in a weekend of drama in October, 1948. St Catherine's school headmaster and local historian, S. McVeigh, is second from the right. The society disbanded in 1950, when the McVeighs left the district.

West Drayton Boys' Club Dramatic Society after their production of *The Younger Generation* at St Catherine's school in November 1946, with producer Leslie R. Boon (centre of the back row).

Unity Theatre (West Drayton) in a scene from *Arms and the Man* at St Martin's Hall in 1946. Left to right: Eileen Goodwin, Leslie Boon, Basil Morton, Cynthia Warren, Mary Morton, Noel James, Michael Latimer. Unity operated from 1945 to 1950; founded the West Middlesex Guild of Dramatic Art; and staged drama festivals in West Drayton.

Phoenix Theatre Group celebrating at a social evening at The Swan in 1958. Formed in 1949, Phoenix became the longest running dramatic society in the area, folding in 1979 after staging sixty-nine productions. Many charities benefited from extra performances in Harefield, Uxbridge, Hillingdon, Southall and Richings Park. From 1958 to 1970, the group won twenty-one drama festivals, and represented West Drayton at Henley, Corby, Thame, Maidenhead, Ruislip, High Wycombe and Harpenden in finals of the British Drama League. Phoenix also presented premieres of the plays *Vacant in August* and *Sink or Swim* at the Women's Institute Hall in 1963 and 1964, both being attended by the respective authors Anthony Booth and Doris Green. Subsequently, *Vacant in August* won five 'Spotlight' awards (sponsored by the *Hayes Chronicle*) for the producer and four cast members.

Cast and backstage crew of *The Soldier and the Woman*, presented by Phoenix at the WI Hall in December, 1966. The shepherd boy third from the right is Russell Grant – now a celebrated astrologer, and next to him is Lyn Stevens, who married one of the Tremeloes pop group, the late Alan Blakley.

Cast and crew of Phoenix's production of *The Cell* at West Drayton Community Centre in February 1973.

Yiewsley and West Drayton Arts Council's Nativity production *Ding Dong Merrily on High* at St Martin's church in December, 1968. Produced by Andrew Low, it was a joint venture involving many local groups. After three performances in St Martin's, the play went 'on tour' to Christ Church with St Barnabas, Marylebone, and St Alban's, Holborn.

Another Arts Council presentation – the pageant 'Fantasia Gloriana' staged in the grounds of Drayton Hall in the summer of 1972. Based on the visit of Queen Elizabeth I to West Drayton, this scene shows the Queen (Kay Fagg) borne aloft in a procession led by Angela Kennedy and Andrea Platford. Producer Andrew Low comes next, followed by Gordon Platford. Many of the cast were also members of the XXV Club Players, who presented outdoor performances of Shakespeare in the grounds of The Old House and Southlands.

Eleven

Spiritual Needs

St Martin's church, West Drayton. The present building dates from the mid-fifteenth century, although a church has stood on the site for at least 800 years. Much restoration work was carried out during the past seventy-five years, mostly involving the tower and interior. In May 1930, a host of theatre celebrities attended the wedding here of C. Aubrey Smith's only daughter Honor to Lt. Commander R. Cobb, RN.

Revd Arthur William Septimus Albert Row, vicar of St Martin's from 1889 to 1928 – the longest incumbency in the church's history. He married a Yiewsley girl at St Matthew's church in 1890, and had one son. Revd Row died at Chelsea in 1931, and is buried in St Martin's churchyard.

St Martin's in deep mid-winter during the early 1930s. The clock on the tower has long since gone.

St Martin's vicar Revd Leslie E. Prout with Mrs Prout and local historian A.H. Cox at the vicarage in April 1948. Revd Prout served the parish from 1928 until his death in 1956, and was a member of the Urban District Council during the 1930s.

St Martin's vicar Revd A.H. Woodhouse, who succeeded Revd Prout in 1956. During his ministry, a new vicarage was built in 1960, and later a new church school (opened by the Duchess of Kent), and parish hall (opened by actor Derek Nimmo). Revd Woodhouse left St Martin's in 1970 and became the Archdeacon of Hereford.

Father Thomas Dunphy, who took charge of St Catherine's Roman Catholic church, West Drayton, on 4 May 1908, but waited ten years before being officially appointed parish priest in December 1919. He died in 1925, his ministry spanning seventeen years in total.

The familiar figure of Father Dunphy in his favourite spot at the gates of St Catherine's opposite The Green during the early 1920s. He became well known to all the villagers as he passed the time of day with everyone who came by.

Monsignor John M.T. Barton, a convert from the Anglican faith, became parish priest at St Catherine's in 1938. Educated at Harrow, he spoke several languages, his favourite being Hebrew. He moved to Westminster in 1950, where he was appointed as a Diocesan Censor of books on Catholicism.

St Catherine's in 1968. The church was established by Father Michael Wren who came to West Drayton on 29 September 1867. The laying of the foundation stone in 1868, the opening of the church in 1869 and its consecration in 1893 all took place on 29 September – the feast of St Michael, Father Wren's patron saint.

Prebendary F.W. Ruffle, was appointed vicar of St Matthew's on 18 January 1938, and retired on 30 September 1973 – thus becoming the longest serving minister in the parish's history. From 1957 to 1967, Revd Ruffle was the Rural Dean of Uxbridge.

St Matthew's church, High Street, Yiewsley was consecrated on 6 July 1859 as a chapel of ease. At that time, Yiewsley was part of Hillingdon parish and did not become a separate civil parish until 1874. Then congregations grew so rapidly that a much enlarged church was re-consecrated by the Bishop of London on 25 April 1898.

Cardinal John Heenan, Archbishop of Westminster, at the grave of Father Michael Wren in St Martin's churchyard on 12 July 1965. On his left is St Catherine's parish priest Father J. McVeigh, and Revd Woodhouse is on the extreme right.

Revd Woodhouse and the Cardinal walking to the church where they prayed together – taking Church unity a step further. Later, Cardinal Heenan described the graveside visit as 'the highlight of his journey to West Drayton'.

Revd E.W. Stenlake, minister of West Drayton Baptist church from 1902 to 1916, and his wife.

The former Baptist chapel in Money Lane. Opened in June 1827, the last service was held on 28 December 1924. The building is now a private residence named Frays House and its outward appearance is unchanged.

The replacement Baptist chapel in Swan Road. Designed by local architect Hubert Bateman and built by his father Samuel, the church opened in 1925. A stone laid by Revd Stenlake in 1924 is incorporated in the frontage.

Side and rear view of the former Yiewsley Baptist Tabernacle, Colham Avenue. It opened in 1900 when the avenue was known as Ernest Road, and was sold in 1954 for commercial purposes.

The foundation stone of a new Baptist Sunday school being laid in July 1934 at the other end of Colham Avenue.

The new Yiewsley Baptist church, also at the other end of the avenue. Opened in September 1955, it replaced both the Tabernacle and the Sunday school building.

The former Wesleyan chapel, High Street, Yiewsley, now restored and converted into offices. Methodists worshipped here until 1927 when the Middlesex County Council purchased the building for use as a library. After a new library opened in 1973 further along the High Street, the former chapel operated as a Youth Centre.

Councillor W. Roberts performing the opening ceremony of the new Wesleyan chapel or Methodist Central Hall, Fairfield Road, Yiewsley, on 31 August 1927. Many celebrated speakers, including journalist Hannen Swaffer and the 'Red Dean' Dr Hewlett Johnson addressed packed congregations here during the 1930s. The hall which was also used for music and band concerts was demolished and replaced by a smaller building in 1973.

Samuel Thorn, a Yiewsley councillor and leading light in the Salvation Army during the 1920s and 1930s. The Army began its work in Yiewsley in 1886, meeting first in a building in the brickfields and then in a large barn that could accommodate 250 people. In 1914 a new permanent citadel was opened in Horton Road, but in recent years it was continually vandalised and finally destroyed by an arson attack.

Yiewsley Salvation Army Band in 1929. Samuel Thorn is second from the left in the middle row, and other members in the picture are George King, Tom and John MacGowan, Charlie Bradley, Archie Roberts, Tommy Taylor, Jim Dowsett, Joe Priest, Will Evans and William Beare.

Twelve
The Sound of Music

Yiewsley Prize Band in 1904. Formed in August 1890 at the Wesleyan chapel, it was originally called the Wesleyan Band of Hope Brass Band and subsequently underwent many name changes. Its longest serving conductors were A.W. Allen (1911-1936) and George Turner (1937-1955). Winners of countless trophies throughout its long history, the band's golden years were during the 1930s and 1940s.

The junior branch of the band in Army Cadet uniform in 1942. Formed by conductor Turner in 1940, they joined as a unit, playing at numerous military functions, concerts and fêtes throughout the Second World War. The senior band had broken up for the duration and so the youngsters kept its name alive until hostilities ended.

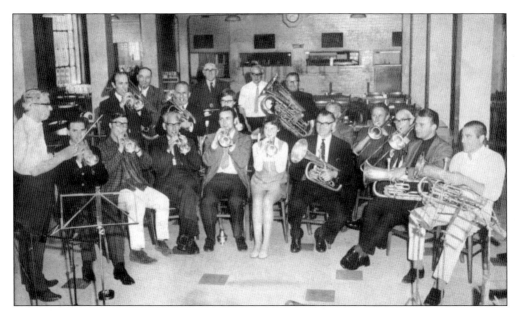

Yiewsley & West Drayton Band Practice at the Anglo Swiss Screw Company in 1969. Managing director Mr F. Frey was the band's president. Fred Outen is conducting and among the personnel are Harry Chandler, Peter Caiger, George Colman, Arthur Hards, Tom Evans, Ted Holland, Bill Spackman and Ken Dixon (who chalked up forty-eight years with the band from 1941 to 1989).

The band in 1971. It was a family tradition for several generations of local people to join the band, among them the Chandlers, Warringtons, Emertons and Leatherbys. Also more youngsters were getting involved, as this picture shows.

The band at a concert in the new Yiewsley Methodist church hall in 1976. Fifth from the left in the back row is Ron McKenzie (principal cornettist and bandmaster for thirty years from 1969 to 1999). His son Paul and daughter Tracy are first and third from the left in the middle row.

West Drayton's Arthur Caiger (known as 'The Man in the White Suit') chatting with King George VI at the FA Cup Final in 1947. The King asked Arthur if the crowd had been in good voice, and when he replied 'Very much so', the King's response was 'Good, because they haven't had much to sing about lately!'

Arthur conducting the 100,000 capacity crowd in Community Singing before the kick-off at Wembley Stadium in 1947.

West Drayton dance band – the 'Sid Johnson Swingtette' playing at the Tower Arms, Richings Park in 1947. Left to right: T. Johnson, S. Johnson, R. Johnson, D. Williams and B. Moores.

Another local band, 'The Draytonaires' who played at dances during the 1950s. Among the line-up were leader W. Twomey (accordion), T. Marshall (piano), W. Goddard (drums) and P. Carter (clarinet).

The 'Pennyblacks' pop group of West Drayton youngsters, who played at discos during the 1960s. Left to right: J. Axtell, T. Marshall Jnr, P. Maher, J. Goodenough and D. Arnold. In later years, T. Marshall turned professional, guesting with Buck's Fizz and other well-known groups.

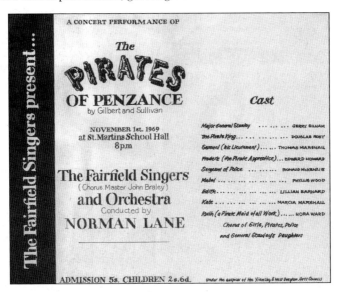

Programme for the Fairfield Singers' production of *The Pirates of Penzance* in 1969. Formed in 1943 under the name Yiewsley, West Drayton & District Choral Society, their president for many years was Arthur Caiger. The society was renamed Fairfield Singers when it began rehearsing at the Central Hall, Fairfield Road, and eventually became the Fairfield Choral Society (since disbanded).

Thirteen
People and
Personalities

Reunion of a well-known Yiewsley family pictured in front of their home in Winnock Road, c. 1912. Mr and Mrs Crockett (seated in centre) had twelve children, all of whom are in the photograph. Left to right, back row: Beatrice, Bill, Rose, Arthur, Nell, Winifred, Jim. Front row: Ruby, Eliza, James, Rebecca, Fred, Alice, Nancy.

C. Aubrey Smith with his wife Isabel at West Drayton Cricket Club Jubilee Fair on Saturday 6 July, 1935. He lived in West Drayton from 1903, having joined the club a year earlier. Previously he played for Sussex for thirteen years, three as captain, and in 1887/88 he toured Australia with the Test side. A year later he captained the first English team to play in South Africa. While living in West Drayton he pursued a stage career in the West End and on Broadway, before settling in Hollywood in 1930. He became known internationally in classic films *Clive of India, Romeo and Juliet, Lloyds of London, The Prisoner of Zenda* and *The Hurricane*, and returned frequently to England to visit his old club and friends. Awarded the CBE in 1938, and knighted in 1944, he died in Beverly Hills in 1948, aged eighty-five.

William Nigel Bruce, second son of Baronet Sir William Bruce, lived at No. 1 De Burgh Crescent from 1905. He joined West Drayton Cricket Club in 1912 with his older brother Michael, and after service with the Somerset Light Infantry in the First World War (in which he was severely wounded) made his stage debut in 1920 – evidently encouraged by his team mate, C.A. Smith. In 1924 they appeared together in *The Creaking Chair* at the Vaudeville, after which Nigel acted regularly in the West End and on Broadway. Film contracts followed and in 1934, he moved to Hollywood. He is best remembered for his portrayals of bumbling Dr Watson in fourteen Sherlock Holmes films opposite Basil Rathbone from 1939 to 1946. He and C. Aubrey appeared in only two films together, but continued their cricketing careers in the Hollywood team founded by CAS in 1931. Nigel died in 1953.

George Thomas Moore Marriott (known professionally as Moore Marriott) was born at Alpha Place, High Street, Yiewsley, on 14 September 1885. Coming from a music-hall family, he made his stage debut at the age of five. After war service in the First World War he worked on stage and in silent films as a leading man, but when talkies arrived decided to specialise in character parts. He appeared in over 300 films, and is best remembered as the stooge to Will Hay and Graham Moffat in classic comedies *Oh, Mr Porter*, *Convict 99*, *Ask a Policeman* and *Where's That Fire?* After retiring in 1948 he kept a grocery shop in Bognor Regis, but died soon afterwards in December, 1949, aged sixty-four.

Henry Havelock Ellis who lived at Woodpecker Farm, Mill Road, West Drayton from 1911 to 1913. A prolific writer on the psychology of sex, he was one of the most controversial figures of his day. His wife Edith, also a writer, wrote a play *The Subjection of Kezia* in which Beryl Faber (Mrs Cosmo Hamilton) appeared in 1908, while she herself was living at nearby 'Southlands'.

Hubert Frank Bateman LRIBA (Licentiate Royal Institute British Architects), on the left of the picture, with colleagues W. Devonshire and G. Hockley in 1938. A founder member and the first chairman of West Drayton History Society – a position he held for six years – Mr Bateman was an architect whose work can still be seen in the area, particularly in Swan Road and at 1 Warwick Road, where he lived. A gifted artist, he will also be remembered for his extremely long service with Yiewsley, West Drayton and Harmondsworth Fire Brigades.

J.W. (Jack) Hearne, Middlesex and England cricketer in his garden at Bagley Close, West Drayton. Probably the greatest of the 'Cricketing Hearnes', Jack joined the Lord's ground staff in 1906. In a most distinguished career, he scored 37,252 runs including ninety-six centuries, and took 1,839 wickets. He represented England in twenty-four Tests, retiring in May 1936, aged forty-five. Coaching and talent spotting followed before he moved to West Drayton, where, according to his son Jack Junior, he enjoyed one of the happiest times of his life. He was a vice-president of West Drayton Cricket Club (his son's club), until his death in September 1965.

Dame Kathleen Lonsdale DBE, FRS, D. Sc. (1903-1971) was professor of chemistry and head of crystallography at University College, London. A prominent Quaker and broadcaster, she lived for many years in De Burgh Crescent, Station Road, opposite the library.

Archibald Henry Cox (known to everyone locally as Archie), lived in West Drayton from 1929 until his death in 1995. From 1934 to 1959 he was secretary of St Martin's parish council and a sidesman for fifty years. A founder member of the history society in 1949, and its chairman from 1955 to 1983, Archie was the town's foremost historian and wrote several books about the district. He was elected an Honorary Member of the London & Middlesex Archaeological Society in 1975, and an Associate of the Royal Historical Society in 1955.

Maurice Bawtree (on the right of the picture) lived in West Drayton from 1920 until his death in 1985. A well-known historian and member of four local history societies, he was mentioned in despatches for distinguished conduct in the RAF from 1939-1945. He was an expert on heraldry, canals and waterways, and the picture shows him with Andrew Low examining a human skull excavated at Iver, Buckinghamshire.

S.A.J. McVeigh lived in West Drayton from 1930 when he was appointed head of St Catherine's Roman Catholic school on 8 September. A founder member of the history society, he wrote two books on the area, published in 1950 and 1970. He moved to Reading in April 1950 to become head of St James's school, but his interest in West Drayton history continued until his death in 1979, after which a third book was published posthumously.

Lena Herod, a Yiewsley resident for sixty years, was secretary of the Hillingdon Arts Association for over twenty-five years, and it became her life's work. A member of 'Hillingdon Writers', she was a prime mover in setting up the Hayes Beck Theatre and Uxbridge Music Festivals, while serving as secretary to the Uxbridge Guild of Arts. She died in 2002.

Arthur Caiger, DSM (Distinguished Service Medal) in the white suit that was his trademark, with his granddaughter Laura at his Swan Road home in 1956. Arthur moved there from Yiewsley in 1927 with his wife Margueritte Williams, a local singer and former soprano with the d'Oyly Carte Opera Company. A headmaster at schools in Lambeth and Clerkenwell, he began his community singing career at RAF Uxbridge, and for twenty-one years conducted concerts nationwide, attended by over 5,000,000 people. From 1947 to 1962 he led the singing at every FA Cup Final at Wembley, in addition to internationals and other matches staged at the stadium. He died in 1964.

Professor A.F. Johns, who lived at Gothic Villas, Swan Road, was probably the best known music teacher in the district. His pre-war prospectus advertised instruction on piano, violin, viola, cello, mandolin, guitar, banjo, flute, piccolo and voice production, at fees ranging from one to three guineas for a term of thirteen lessons. Pupils were tutored at his home with others who studied general subjects, and throughout the war years, he gave lessons at the Boys' Club until he was forced to retire in 1945 due to ill-health. From 1935 to 1939, Professor Johns also served as a churchwarden at St Martin's.

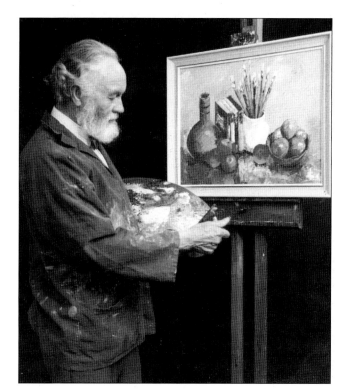

West Drayton artist Leslie Nind at work. Leslie, assisted by his wife Joan, was the driving force behind the formation of the Arts Council in 1963, and the setting up of the Arts Centre at Southlands. Since then, the Ninds have worked ceaselessly to ensure the centre's success, for which they were honoured by an award from the Hillingdon Arts Association in 1987.

Sir Allen Lane signing the visitors' book at the opening of Southlands Arts Centre in 1967. Sir Allen, founder of Penguin Books, was knighted in 1952. The first president of the Yiewsley & West Drayton Arts Council, he lived at Old Mill House, West Drayton, from the early 1960s until his death in 1970.

127

Julian Rhind-Tutt, member of a well-known West Drayton family, is currently establishing himself in the world of theatre and television. After training at the Central School of Speech & Drama, he spent some years at the National, playing in *The Way of the World*, *Richard II* and *The Madness of King George III*. More recently he appeared in the films *The Madness of King George*, *Notting Hill*, *Les Misérables* and *Tomb Raider*. On television he reprised his role in *Richard II*, and acted in *Avenging Angels*, *The Heat of the Sun*, *An Unsuitable Job for a Woman*, *Hippies*, *The Wilsons* and *Reckless*. In 1992, he received the Carleton Hobbs award from the BBC.

West Drayton actress Carla Mendonca was formerly a neighbour of Philip Rhind-Tutt and, like him, gained a BA (Hons) degree at Warwick University. Making her theatre debut in 1985 at the Globe in *Daisy Pulls It Off*, she then played in various repertory companies nationwide. In recent years she has worked almost exclusively in television, appearing with Lenny Henry, Brian Conley, Hale and Pace, Smith and Jones and French and Saunders.